Desertedplateau

KATHERINE STINSON

BookLeaf
Publishing

India | USA | UK

Presentation by *BookLeaf Publishing*

Web: www.bookleafpub.com

E-mail: info@bookleafpub.com

ISBN: 9789360944025

First edition 2024

For Dr. Alvarez Hughes, who inspired me to embrace my inner gem and share my writing with the world.

ACKNOWLEDGEMENT

In bringing this book to life, I've been blessed with the unwavering support of incredible souls who've left their mark on every page with love.

To BookLeaf Publishing, your challenge wasn't just a task; it was a doorway to creativity. Thank you for providing the platform that turned mere words into a living, breathing collection.

To my family and friends, you've been my rocks on this writing adventure. Your unyielding belief in me and your unwavering support when climbing "that goddamn mountain" have made this journey truly special. I write these words with the ink of your love.

To the boys who've been a part of my life's story—thank you for being the heartbeat in my pen, even in moments of heartbreak and loss. Your presence has colored the emotional depth of these verses.

Jared Singer, your suggestion to play with new compound words became the title of my book.

To Doula of Words, those tear-inducing free-writing moments were pure magic.

Dr. Alvarez-Hughes, your encouragement to publish that first poem set me on this path. I write with gratitude for your belief in the potential of my words.

Marina Williams for editing my poetry.

And to Sabrina Benaim, your guidance in that first poetry workshop was a grounding force. Every line in this book is because I took my first step in your workshop.

This isn't just a book; it's a collective labor of love, a shared journey of hearts and words. To everyone who has contributed, your love is the invisible thread that binds this creation. Here's to the authenticity of the human experience—raw, genuine, and filled with love.

PREFACE

In the rhythmic pulse of a 21-day challenge, where the commitment to daily creation met the familiarity of cherished verses, this poetry collection was born. Here lies a tapestry woven from both the threads of well-loved favorites and the freshly inked lines that unfolded with each passing day.

The decision to intertwine previously written poems with the new was a deliberate choice—an acknowledgment of the beauty that resides in both continuity and spontaneity. Each poem, whether a familiar friend or a newfound creation, carries the weight of authenticity and a piece of my ever-evolving soul.

Some verses were plucked from the archives of personal favorites, like old letters revisited and cherished anew. They stand as timeless witnesses to the emotions that linger, persisting beyond the bounds of a single moment. Others, born fresh and unbridled in the crucible of daily commitment, encapsulate the raw immediacy of the present—a snapshot of my mind in perpetual motion.

This collection is a testament to the duality of creativity—a dance between the comfort of the known and the exhilaration of the undiscovered. As you traverse these pages, may you find resonance in the familiar cadence of treasured poems and the vibrant energy that radiates from the uncharted verses.

To those who joined me on this poetic sojourn, whether through the embrace of old lines or the discovery of new ones, I extend my heartfelt gratitude. It is my hope that within these words, you'll find a reflection of your own journey, an invitation to savor the beauty of both continuity and change.

Birds of a Feather Flock Together

Galapagos Finches go through speciation, just as we did. Separated by distance became the norm for us. The gentle "see you laters" collided and collapsed into the unspoken but felt "goodbyes." You started out as the "right one," but this was the beginning of another end. A peacock widens feathers to show their true colors as you showed yours; no longer representing beauty in my eyes, the beholder. Instead, a vulture, "Nature's Garbage Man," molded into reality. I was fresh meat seen instantly like a flock of ugly souls waiting to wake together. First watching me get devoured from a distance, then turning into scavengers searching for the right moment to dive down deep together in order to feed on carcass. Love is like death. It is reincarnated.

Masquerade

Masquerade
There is no past I
need to go back to

No bones that need collecting
along with validation

       from those who haunted and
     pretended to wipe my tears

They created them

I'll never let them see that part of me

A hard shell
A mushy inside

How dare you judge me
You tried kissing me, before saying
"Hello"

There's no mask you get to release
A masquerade ball is my forte

I just move

forward

Baby steps

Stretching out to be
the woman I already am

You don't get to know who I want to be

My hopes and desires
                                float
away

I don't slam the door on you,
but I whisper to myself

"He's not even who the old me
dreamed of."

Ways in Which a Woman is a WITCH on Tinder

-	A recurring nightmare sends phones into shock. Fuzzed out, blurred out, click to reveal the picture. Worse than a full moon. Attached reads, "Now you owe me."

-   The perfect disappearing act exists—one block button and a first taste of self-love. Sexier than any view of the sky.

-	"No, I will not go to church with you. I am busy summoning demons."
-	"Ouija" is my middle name, with a capital O.
-	Long, open to short questions, it's contradicting, all of a sudden made into Bridezilla.
-	A boy cancels a date, and suddenly like Evanescence they think they can see into your eyes like open doors. "You're not in the mood for company," they text.

-	Woman's Roman Empire is Salem Witch Trials, ways to torture, defeat, and destroy. Rather be burned at the stake than abused for burning your steak.

-        When told, "I tell everyone you're my woman," the fair response is "You're not my boyfriend, I have thousands of boyfriends."
They respond back with "Well, I do not care, you're my woman". Bitch slapped and my final words, "I didn't put a spell on you, you are not mine."

-        Psycho if standards aren't lowered and accept that they're looking for friends. Define friends—friends with benefits; benefits without friends; friends without benefits.

-        You don't ask me out, I will take myself on a date.

-        The Apothecary shop is not for you. I do not need you to love me. I do not need to kill you; you are already dead inside. It's a secret spot where magical things happen, for me.

-        Intimidating: Resting Bitch Face. Swipe Left.

-        Feminist: She's a man hater, liberal loving, snowflake. Left winged, left swipe.

-        Independent: OH, she doesn't need a man, she can't be controlled. Left, right, left, right, LEFT.

-        Strong: Powerful, bigger than me. I might have to man up. Left on read.

-        "I must not be your top priority; you aren't answering my messages in .5 seconds." Pops up for the 99th time—automatically unmatched.

-        Denied his Facetime call.

-        "Wanna fuck?" as his opener. Reply with "Yeah, fuck you up."

-        The date is late, your carriage already turned into a Jack-O-Lantern.

-        "You're such a bitch, you're CrAAzy, you're too much." Correct that male with, "I am a Goddamn Witch."

WARNING- TINDER IS NOT FOR THE TENDER HEARTED

Alternatives

I am here. I would send you a Daily Duck, but you'll just respond with your typical lol. Not even all CAPS, no HAHA or laughing/crying emoji. You never give an inch, there is a possibility you would give a mile.
I am here and would hold you tight, but your chemo ports are delicate. You come across as strong and emotionless, but I saw the twinkle leave your eyes when you double checked for a clean towel.
I am here and I love you. It is uncertain to what extent, maybe it comes out in the ocean I wish in or the prayer wall at the jewelry store. Maybe it is spoken in the Malachite I purchased for you in Bali. It is apparent on the "Cure Lymphoma" picture on my vision board.
My tears no longer tasted salty as they streamed down my face when you spoke of Stage 4 cancer. They now taste of hope, magic, and "Please if there is a god, heal this man. Even if he will never love me, he is needed. Whoever loves him in the future, or maybe now, needs him here."
I am here and I am not going anywhere.
And neither are you.

Happiness is a Sound

I remember I got my hearing aids at age 34. It was summer, July. Taking over a month to receive them. I swear my hearing was worse during that time. I'd been without assisted ears my entire life. Why worse, now?
I remember hearing the clarity of my mother's rather loud voice for the first time. I could understand the pronunciation of my name, Katherine. My eyes, puffy, and wet. I repeated it back—"Katherine."
I remember the first song I played on Spotify: Taylor Swift's, "Champagne Problems." The most beautiful Oompah piano. I could finally hear. What was music for me in the past? I replayed and shuffled through songs for 5 hours. I'd been deprived of it all these years. My dance moves now move to more than just a beat.
I remember before hearing devices, I hated humming, hearing humming. I could feel humming, raging through my veins. Well, humming I still do not like you.
I remember learning that laughter has a sound. In Uganda, children were singing. That was the definition of happiness. Smiles taking over their faces. Eyes crinkled. That's how you know

someone is truly happy. Their dance moves were added to it. I boogied along to the sound, the sound of joy.

I remember noticing that office doors squeak, paper ruffles, and footsteps occupy much of the doctor's office. "Will I be overwhelmed in real life?", I said. To this day, it doesn't bother me. There is joy in every sound. I will not take it for granted.

I remember going on walks outside, every day. I just wanted to hear the nature. The flutter of the butterflies' wings, the whispers I made to the dandelions, the crunch of the grass below my feet. Even clouds make a sound as they change shape.

I remember getting goosebumps for the first time after I had my BI Cross. Those too, made a sound. As they appeared, shot through my entire being, stuck up every hair, my skin shriveled up and told a story of the moment my emotions took over.

I remember I can mute my ears now, when a baby cries, grandpa snores, or the gossip in the women's restroom is much too cruel. Why would I want to miss out on these? I'll calm the baby, rub my grandfather's back until he's settled, and tell the girls they are beautiful.

Small Things Worth Celebrating: After Amy Kay

Buying a plane ticket to escape emotional abuse from a pilot that never figured out how to navigate his own life yet tries to control yours. Catching your first wave. Being kissed on the forehead by someone that adores you. Singing your heart out at Bruce Springsteen's concert in May of 2012. Getting your makeup done to impress yourself. Laughing until you piss in your britches. Cats purring. Smooth legs brought to you by yours truly, Coochy. A day at Complexion, gossiping with your esthetician. Hugs from tiny humans even when they're covered in glue. Napping at your best friend's house while she watches *The Boy*. The final relief of an itch. Watermelon running down your face while in Ocean Springs, Mississippi. Sonic's cherry limeade slushies. Women's poetry courses. The sensation you feel when you cannon ball into the pool on the first day of summer. Convertible hair. Purchasing all the dresses from Lulu's. Memorizing the lyrics to your new favorite jam. Leonardo DiCaprio. Curling up in the winter with your grandmother's wool blanket. Booging down to

80s music. Glitter, sparkles, and shimmer galore!
Cabin Fever's "pancakes, pancakes!!!!!"
Knowing everything will work out. Overcoming
your hurdles. Not letting your silk comforter
slide off the bed while sharing your bed with a
mystery. Chocolate milkshakes that don't give
you the runs. It's rare so embrace it. The meeting
of a pleasant stranger. A work week that passes
in the blink of an eye. Cheering your friends on.
Loving more than you could ever imagine.
Sharing that love so much love that nobody has
ever been used to being loved so much.
Popsicles in The Netherlands. Sneezes,
particularly four in a row. Nothing beats the
tickle even with snot pouring out your nostrils.
Bawling while watching Life as a House for the
200th time. Making it to the top of the Rainbow
Mountains. Feeling needed. Surviving the school
year. Walking away from a toxic relationship.
Naps. All the naps. Different skin-colored
crayons. Standing up for what you believe in.
Not having to wear a bra. The "Oh, yaaaaah"
from your past. Big Foot, Lochness Monster,
and Chupacabra—daydreaming about their
existence. Sunflowers that cover France. Pimple
patches. The sound of nails typing. Music and
Rhythm. Tenderness. Connection. Courage.
Psychics that are wrong. You never want a
psychic to predict your actual future. It ruins the

fun. Fully charged phones. Waking up with no
alarm.

The fact that the sun will rise again.

The unknown of what the tide will bring.

Theodore John

Almond blue eyes,

Sparkling with innocent truths

Wavy, gapped tooth lips

Forming new and unusual squeaks

Speak the necessary truth:

"You are beautiful."

Shrimp Butts

As we sit around the perfectly round dinner table with crisp, freshly folded napkins around it, we all think of the answer to the same question. "What would you like to eat?" The Four-Cousin Squad consists of pimply, knuckleheads and one practically a baby. The youngest. We give each other shifty eyes as the blonde waitress pierces us with her ice blue glare. She licks her lips impatiently as she takes not one, but six orders from a family on vacation in the Big Apple. We get to the littlest cousin, and we see a bubble form in his cheeks like a squirrel collecting acorns. He's about to burst. Flushed cheeks, teary eyes...a rumble...a roar of laughter pours some saliva out of his mouth. Shrimp Buttssssssss! He bursts into tears. Tears of laughter. It's so contagious. We all catch it. Each of us cracking up harder than the next.

As I sit with the youngest, now the tallest, we talk about how that trip really brought us together. Shrimp Butts will always be an inside joke between close blood relatives. It cracks the Four-Cousin Squad up in an instant and reconnects us no matter how far apart we are in proximity or emotionally. That memory we shared stays the same. The same ages, the same experiences, and the same tone of laughter. Nothing separates these kin during the remembrance of Shrimp Butts at a Chinese restaurant in the middle of New York City.

The story fills me with warmth and joy. I feel fuzzy inside. A smile sneaks across my face. I grasp onto my chest, close down my eyes, and feel it. I feel the energy from my heart to my cousins' hearts. We are in rhythm. We aren't questioning anything. We stop and look. Look at each other and come to our adult senses that this is family.

This is love. This is love. This IS love.

Letter of Last Instruction:
After Amy Kay

When I die, light up the night sky with fireflies.
Take my ashes and spread them among the
wildflowers. Chant remarkable stories, over and
over again to the people who need to hear them
most.

When I die, catch a wave for me. Envision I am
there with you, learning for the first time. Bust a
move to "Dancing in the Moonlight" and praise
the eternal night light for life comes in phases,
just as it does. Remember that. Skip the nitty
gritty and get to the good stuff: acceptance.
Celebrate my life, but more importantly yours.
Do not wallow in sorrows. Take care of each
other. Write poems and spread them like
wildfires, but keep mine in a sacred spot.
Obsess over something. Truly find a passion
until it runs dry. Find a new passion. Repeat.
Drink Vodka Redbulls out of the Shark Cup I got
in Biloxi. Take me with you when you create
new memories.

When I die, make sure you love again.
If you need me, fly above 17.316010,
-87.535103. Bring a camera, cause boy there's a
sight to see. When I die, that's where I will be.

Bob

Pop.
Palindrome.
He's the same no matter the circumstances.
Every. Which. Way.
Through "The Streak."
Through the sheet forts on the round bed.
Millionaire at heart.
Taught me to be wild, free.
Beyond loving.
Can not bury your money.
Die with a full heart.
Rich people don't leave Muleshoe.
Heck, not even the nursing home.
Swims across the ocean to become the oldest.
Boy Scout.
Always breaking a world record.
Used to be the last hand I wanted to hold.

Now I choose it over anyone's.

I jump. He jumps. Skydiving.
Only a stint to stop him.

One eye always open. Lurking.
It's glass.

He takes his eye out.
Who does that?

My father's

Dad.

Heinz Sight 20/20

Ketchup. A condiment consuming 97% of
American homes.
A stained accessory to all of my outfits.
A permanent resident to my fingerprints.
An escape artist.
A tomato-based sugary napalm.
A french fry's luscious lipstick.
A perfect cover up for a period blotch.
A sweet, sour, bitter, salty, and savory explosion.
An evil, awful, childish food.
A stench of desperation.
A mom's cheap fingerpaint. Just add mustard.
A disaster to the Dutch, clogging arteries, not
feet.
Catsup.
Heinz.
The best thing that comes to those who do not
eat.

Refresh

Stunted growth.
Nah, she's just tiny.
95-pound weakling, her mom teased.
Bikini bottoms. In public. Not an option.
Cellulite, stubble, dear god a camel toe slip.
All the reasons to hide imperfections consumed
her.
95 shrinks to 85 and suddenly there was no
teasing.
Losing weight became reinforced with
compliments by people who did not matter.
Stress was the easiest cover up. Just a white lie.
Tangerine colored skin painted over the
curvature of her body hid any body hair that was
missed by all the razors and waxes.
Defined her Wanna-Be abs.
Body Contouring.
Body sculpting.
Accufit.
She was just "experimenting" to see if they…
actually worked.
Today she decided.
Strip away fake tans. Contour her mind instead
of her breathing sculpture. Shaping the way she
thinks about herself.

Drops her trousers unleashing her newest bikini
bottom.
Quickly, a reflex begins sliding her boardshorts
back to cover herself.
Then.
All the negative thoughts are simply washed
away.
Crockett Waterfall is a sign of rebirth bringing
clarity to a person who is spiritual,
yet questions religion.
Instead of tears streaming down her sunburned
face, fresh, clear water trickles over her head
symbolizing purification.
A Baptism out of the ordinary.
It does not bring her closer to God, but closer to
herself.
A new relationship with her body forms as
insecurity disappears among nature's freedom.
She is no longer caged by doubt. The curse
brought on by society and herself has
disintegrated by Holy Water replenishing the
spring.
Refresh: "give new strength or energy to;
reinvigorate."

DOES THE DEW DO IT?

Cousins. Taco Bell. KFC.
Baja Blast. Typhoon. Code Red. Distortion
Freeze. Sweet Lightning.
Mysterious for reason of long distance.
Distinctive in which they're all hyped up on
Mountain Dew—as seen on Talladega Nights.
Each an artist. Handsome with fantastic
eyebrows and a jawline that wouldn't hurt a fly.
Each visit they become less strangers.
More a warm hug.
My last memory, before this one: 5 glasses of
Mountain Dew at Frisch's Big Boy.
This visit. Discovering the psychology of
wrapping arms around each other.
Four arms raised high. They surrendered.
Holding tight enough to give the
impression that beyond Cars. Art. Band. Movies.
Games.
There are 2 big hearts that pump love, blood,
and the newest MD through their veins.
I would not change it for the world.

Becomes

I am 34.
Been the same size since I was 12.
Or maybe before.
I am not sure.
Do not remember.
What I do remember is standing at Disney
World.
Being introduced to strangers.
I'd smile.
"This is our granddaughter, Katie. Guess how
old she is!"
I've always hated KATIE.
Much too preppy.
They can call me anything.
Grandma. Grandpa.
What's worse than being called by a name that is
more preppy than me?
"Guess how old she is!"
I'm clearly at Disney.
Not clearly, 15.
I've had sex.
These strangers think I'm a KID.
My grandparents
Giggle, giggle
"She is 15."

I will stay the same size, forever.
At age 34 I might look 25 now.
I embrace it as I show my ID to bartenders.
Swipe 24 year olds, yes.

My height will never change
Unless I turn into a Hunchback.
I already have Scoliosis.

My size will always stay 0-2.

I will fluctuate.
No more than the past.
I will get wrinkles.
Frown line Botox will not keep age
Showing in my hands.
My neck. It will go too.
My hair.
She has already changed.
Gray.
I dye her.

What will stay the same along with my size are my
Dance moves.
The amount I love Harry Styles.
The way the ocean feels between my toes.

In life, we change
We grow
We evolve.

I have come to peace with turning 35 this year.

As long as the ocean still feels the same beneath
my feet.

Nights

Sitting here.
Thinking of all the boys who never really loved
me.
They never said they did.
I just wanted time to believe it.
I care for them each.
Is it love? I do not know.
Wanting to unblock them
Just to see if they are there.
Hoping for a "Hello, Katherine."
It will bring me back to the familiar cycle.
The rude awakening comes with
Place fillers, never really there.
I am alone.

Expressions

Canyons across my forehead telling stories of
earthquakes caused by my eyebrows.

The perfect sculptures many paint on, mine are
natural.

Unibrow is the price I pay.

Lioness eyes.
Luscious lashes.
Lids that let me sleep.

A squishy nose.
Rosy touch added to the tips.
Cheeks too.
The color tells the truth.

Peach fuzz across my face reminds me I'm alive.
Goosebumps raise the hairs. How else does one
know what they feel?

My lips whisper not innocent words. I fucking
like that.

A beautiful smile isn't just my pearly whites, but
the crinkles in my eyes.
The lifts of my brows.
The warmth of my heart.

I got it from my granny.

Chin completes my face.
Mine matches my cousin's.

It's beautiful and so am I.

A Letter to Myself

Dear Kat,
You viewed the world with a bandaid tint and
one eye like your grandfather.
Spent the nights in the MRI viewing Lisa Frank
stickers on the ceiling. You counted those
instead of sheep.
You went through life listening with your ears,
but not understanding.
This made you feel alone.
Solitude. Isolation.
The world did not seem to understand you just
as in reality you literally could not understand
62% of things others said.
You relied on people's lips more than you knew.
It wasn't that K did not want to be your friend.
Her father died by suicide.
She was also 5.

I'm writing to tell you, these things passed. You
gotta let go. You stopped wearing the eye patch,
got cute glasses that you never wear. At age 34
you finally got hearing aids. You and the world
finally understand each other. You found new
friends and they love to hear you.

Your inner child is healed and so are you.

Love,
Kate

PB&J

I've had you physically, on call, on your watch.
Scheduled by you.
"Hey, what's up?"
I know what that means.

If I was busy,
You'd wait.
You'd come over when the handy man was
fixing my washer.
You'd wait 2 hours in my hair dresser's
Parking lot
Just to bang for 2 minutes.
I won't give you more credit than that.
I was so mad.
I blocked you.

If you were busy,
I'd be told
"Another time."

I never had you emotionally.
You did not want any sort of connection.
I went along with it.

2.5 years later

Physically Lymphoma.
Stage 4
Is your priority.
I don't blame you.

Instead of waiting for me you spend
6 hours every 2 weeks in Chemotherapy.
At least 5 days healing
You eat a large meal on Fridays or Saturdays
Just to start over again.

Emotionally I still don't have you
Lymphoma does, and your loved ones.
My emotions have changed from wanting to
love you.
I want you to survive.

We chat about the treatment center
And the PBJ sandwiches you hate.
You want treatment to be in sunshine.

You attend the VA, alone,
Nap and watch Netflix.
You want to go through this alone.
Your mom and dad pick you up.

I won't understand until I am sick
And fearing for my life.

All I can do is respect your wishes.

Secretly,
I think you know.
I am here.

Dean's List

The psychiatrist called me his
honorary dean's list
patient.

He put me back on just 2 pills
instead of an entire cocktail menu.
300 mg Lithium and a tiny speck of Abilify,
2mg.

I used to be his poster child patient.
I am not really understanding
how I can be doing
well enough on
a much less dosage than I was before?

He did not even put me back on ALL
the medicine he prescribed in 2011.

Did I need all that?
So long?

All I know is my,
let's call it a mocktail
or maybe even a "shot"
is working better.

It's always in the back of my
mind that it could be hypomania.
What goes up…
Must come down…

That's what my doctor said.

What they don't teach us—
What passion is
What obsession is
What normal is
They just give us a pill.

Yellow Brick Roads

Less than gracefully, thoroughly, filled with no
guilt, devour that spoonful of peanut butter—
you are Joe Black.
Faire Frou Frou for days; glowing, sparkling,
shimmering of the soul. Hum Ho'oponopono to
yourself, on more occasions than not.
Buy yourself a Robert August designed
surfboard from his famous shop in Tamarindo.
Take it out into the wild; practice, never give up,
and enjoy every wave. The ride may only last
seconds, but the feelings will be engraved in
your heart for all time.
Accidentally on purpose venture into France
where the sunflowers are endless. The Yellow
Brick Roads of Reality. They'll take your breath
away, which is what you need. Silence to
envision everything you love, hold onto, and
release. Carefully take a flower from the field;
when you get home, hang it upside down to dry
it out. Keep it. Put it in your European
scrapbook next to your favorite memory.
Put on your oldest pair of Nikes that still read,
"NEVER GIVE UP," and run that race, climb
those hundreds of stairs. You are one with the

Eiffel Tower. "Make time to dance alone with
one hand waving free."
Take it all in and do it all again.

"Make time to dance alone with one hand
waving free." Elizabeth Town.

I Don't Know All the People Who I'll Love Yet

You could be next door.
A mile away.
At Nazare with a heart as big as the waves.
100 ft arm span to hug me with.
Or
I could've swiped your arm in the grocery store.
While picking the perfect mango.
Not too green.
Not too hard.
Not too soft.
I hope you'll be as sweet as a mango.
I hope you'll be a tad juicy.
I hope you'll like the grocery store.
I could've been your pen pal.
Written to you across the 7 seas.
Sealed your envelope with a kiss.
A french kiss.
Maybe I just didn't love you…yet.
I hope I'll meet you in yesterday's tracksuit.
I hope you look at me like Jude Law looks at
Cameron Diaz.
I hope you'll be crossing your own finish line.
13.1 miles ran.
13.1 weeks sober.

13.1 dollars won on a scratch off.

I hope you meet me at my finish line.

13.1 miles I could've ran.

13.1 weeks I've written a love poem.

13.1 dollars I spent wishing on you.

www.ingramcontent.com/pod-product-compliance
Lightning Source LLC
La Vergne TN
LVHW021301200726
843509LV00012B/1743